SUPER
SURPRISING
TRiViA
ABOUT
the WORLD'S NATURAL
WONDERS

by Ailynn Collins

CAPSTONE PRESS
a capstone imprint

Spark is published by Capstone Press, an imprint of Capstone
1710 Roe Crest Drive, North Mankato, Minnesota 56003
capstonepub.com

Library of Congress Cataloging-in-Publication Data is available on the
Library of Congress website.
ISBN: 9781669050476 (hardcover)
ISBN: 9781669071792 (paperback)
ISBN: 9781669050438 (ebook PDF)

Summary: Think you know a lot about Earth's natural wonders? Prepare to
know even more about the world's biggest deserts, tallest mountains, and
deepest canyons. You'll be surprised by how much you'll discover in this
totally terrific book of trivia about natural wonders.

Editorial Credits
Editor: Erika L. Shores; Designer: Heidi Thompson; Media Researcher:
Jo Miller; Production Specialist: Tori Abraham

Image Credits
Getty Images: Anton Litvintsev, 12, Anup Shah, 7 (bottom), aphotostory,
10, Arctic-Images, 18, Draper White, 24, MediaProduction, 11, Onfokus,
29, Pavliha, 7 (top), Stocktrek Images, 6; Shutterstock: Al'fred, 27 (top), Dr
Morley Read, 4, 26, Gigi Peis, Cover (top right), 20, Hollygraphic, (design
element) throughout, ImageBank4u, 21, Invisible Witness, 25, ioanna_alexa,
19 (top), JC Photo, 17 (top), Kabindra shrestha, 22, Lapa Smile, 19 (bottom),
Lorcel, 23, max dallocco, 8, mexrix, (background) throughout, Mike-Hubert.
com, Cover (bottom left), Nowaczyk, 27 (bottom), Ondrej Prosicky, 27
(middle), Ppictures, 15 (bottom), Razi the wandering soul, 14 (bottom),
Robert Marxen, 9, Sanit Fuangnakhon, Cover (bottom right), 28 (bottom),
Scottish Traveller, 14 (top), SCStock, 15 (top), SL-Photography, 28 (top),
Tracey Jones Photography, 16, Vac1, Cover (top left), Vixit, 13, Wagsy, 17
(bottom), Yingna Cai, 5

All internet sites appearing in back matter were available and accurate when
this book was sent to press.

Printed and bound in China. PO5379

TABLE OF CONTENTS

Did You Know? 4

Africa 6

Antarctica. 8

Asia and the Middle East. 10

Australia. 16

Europe 18

North America 22

South America 26

Glossary. 30

Read More 31

Internet Sites 31

Index. 32

About the Author 32

Words in **bold** are in the glossary.

DID YOU KNOW?

Earth is filled with surprising places. Some places have strange giant rocks. Others have forests with trees taller than most buildings. You might even find a place that looks like an alien planet!

One **continent** at a time, let's discover these awesome places.

AFRICA

The Sahara is the world's biggest hot desert.

It is almost the size of the United States.

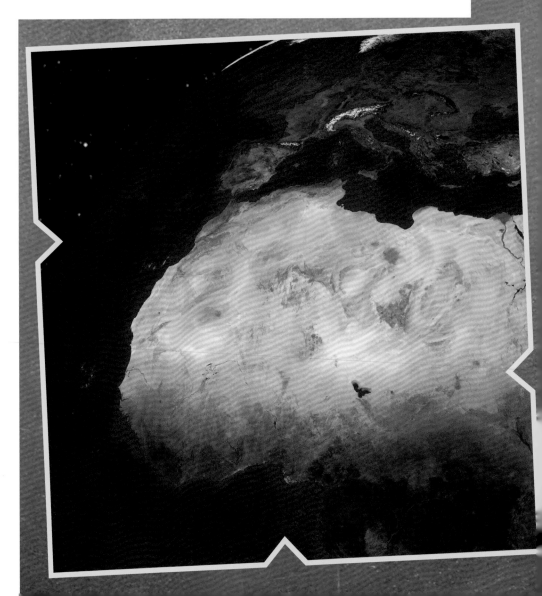

Dust from the Sahara gets blown across the Atlantic Ocean. It reaches the Amazon Rainforest. **Minerals** in the dust help Amazon plants grow.

Every year 1.5 million wildebeest and 200,000 zebras move at least 500 miles from Tanzania to Kenya and back. This is called the Great **Migration**.

ANTARCTICA

Antarctica's ice holds more than half of all the fresh water in the world.

Some of Antarctica's ice has been frozen for 35 million years.

ASIA and the MIDDLE EAST

The Zhangjiajie National Forest Park has 3,000 stone pillars. The tallest is 3,543 feet high.

High in the Zhangjiajie National Forest is the world's longest, highest glass bridge. It's as long as four football fields. It's three times higher than the Statue of Liberty.

The world's oldest lake is Lake Baikal

in Russia. It's 25 to 30 million years old.

Mount Everest is the tallest peak on Earth.

It grows taller by 16 inches every 100 years.

The Al Naslaa rock is in Saudi Arabia. It has been split in two by a perfectly straight crack. Scientists think the ground beneath it moved. That's what caused the crack.

The Wadi Rum desert in Jordan has red sand.

Wadi Rum looks like an alien planet.

Movies about space have been filmed here.

AUSTRALIA

Australia's Great Barrier Reef is the largest living thing on Earth.

The Great Barrier Reef can be seen from space.

More than 600 types of coral
are found in the reef.

EUROPE

The best place to see the Northern Lights is the village of Abisko in Sweden. From October to March, the night sky lights up. It flashes green, purple, blue, red, and yellow.

Tenerife is an island southwest of Spain.
Ten of its beaches have black sand. The sand is
volcanic lava. It's broken down by sea water.

The Giant's **Causeway** is in Ireland. The area looks like a giant made huge rocks shaped like hexagons. But really, they were formed by 60 million years of lava flow and **erosion**.

Iceland has 32 active volcanoes.

At least one erupts every five years.

NORTH AMERICA

Banff National Park in Canada has many **glaciers**. This ice holds tiny bits of rock. When the ice melts, it flows into lakes. The rock powder makes the water look bright blue-green in the sunshine.

At Yellowstone National Park, water springs from deep inside the earth. The Grand Prismatic Spring pushes up more than 560 gallons of very hot water per minute.

The Grand Canyon is carved by wind and water. The Colorado River runs through it. The canyon is still growing.

Dinosaur bones have never been found in the Grand Canyon. The rock is more than a billion years old. But the canyon formed after the dinosaurs lived.

SOUTH AMERICA

The Amazon Rainforest is the world's largest forest. It has 390 billion trees.

Amazon treetops are very close together. It can take a raindrop 10 minutes to reach the forest floor.

The Amazon Rainforest has 2.5 million types of insects.

Salar de Uyuni in Bolivia is the world's biggest salt flat. Every November, pink flamingos lay their eggs here.

When rain falls on the salt, the water makes Salar de Uyuni look like the world's biggest mirror.

Glossary

causeway (KAWZ-way)—a raised road or track that goes over water

continent (KAHN-tuh-nuhnt)—one of Earth's seven large land masses

erosion (i-ROH-zhuhn)—the wearing away of land by water or wind

glacier (GLAY-shur)—a large body of ice moving slowly down a slope or valley or spreading outward on a land surface

migration (mye-GRAY-shuhn)—the movement of people or animals from one region to another

mineral (MIN-ur-uhl)—a material found in nature that is not an animal or a plant

volcanic (vol-KAN-ik)—relating to a volcano

Read More

Bellows, Melina Gerosa. *Totally Random Facts: 3,128 Wild, Wacky, and Wondrous Things About the World*. New York: Bright Matter Books, 2022.

Driggs, Lorin. *Landmarks Around the World*. Huntington Beach, CA: Teacher Created Materials, 2023.

Gifford, Clive. *Our World in Numbers: An Encyclopedia of Fantastic Facts*. New York: DK Publishing, 2022.

Internet Sites

7 Wonders of the World
online.kidsdiscover.com/unit/7-wonders-of-the-world

National Geographic Kids
kids.nationalgeographic.com/

The Seven Natural Wonders of the World
worldatlas.com/places/the-7-natural-wonders-of-the-world.html

Al Naslaa rock, 14
Amazon Rainforest, 7, 26, 27
Antarctica, 8, 9

Banff National Park, 22

Giant's Causeway, 20
Grand Canyon, 24, 25
Grand Prismatic Spring, 23
Great Barrier Reef, 16, 17
Great Migration, 7

Lake Baikal, 12

Mount Everest, 13

Northern Lights, 18

Sahara, the, 6, 7
Salar de Uyuni, 28, 29

Tenerife, 19

volcanoes, 21

Wadi Rum desert, 15

Yellowstone National Park, 23

Zhangjiajie National Forest, 10, 11

About the Author

Ailynn Collins has written many books for children, from stories about aliens and monsters, to books about science, space, and the future. These are her favorite subjects. She has an MFA in writing for children and young adults from Hamline University and has spent many years as a teacher. She lives outside Seattle with her family and six dogs. When she's not writing, she enjoys participating in dog shows and dog sports.